GLADIATORS

Brandon Robshaw
and Rochelle Scholar

Published in association with
The Basic Skills Agency

Hodder & Stoughton

A MEMBER OF THE HODDER HEADLINE GROUP

Acknowledgements
Cover: Jacey
Illustrations: Oisin McGann
Photos: p. 5 © Dreamworks/Universal Pictures from The Ronald Grant Archive; p. 20 © Hugh Rooney/Eye Ubiquitous/CORBIS; p. 26 © Karl Weatherly/CORBIS.

Orders: please contact Bookpoint Ltd, 130 Milton Park, Abingdon, Oxon OX14 4SB. Telephone: (44) 01235 827720, Fax: (44) 01235 400454. Lines are open from 9.00 – 6.00, Monday to Saturday, with a 24 hour message answering service. Email address: orders@bookpoint.co.uk

British Library Cataloguing in Publication Data
A catalogue record for this title is available from The British Library

ISBN 0 340 84864 2

First published 2002
Impression number   10 9 8 7 6 5 4 3 2 1
Year   2007 2006 2005 2004 2003 2002

Copyright © 2002 Brandon Robshaw and Rochelle Scholar

Typeset by SX Composing DTP, Rayleigh, Essex.
Printed in Great Britain for Hodder & Stoughton Educational, a division of Hodder Headline Plc, 338 Euston Road, London NW1 3BH by The Bath Press Ltd.

Contents

		Page
1	Death	1
2	The Games	4
3	How it all began	7
4	Law and Order	9
5	The Professionals	12
6	Wild Animals	16
7	The Colosseum	19
8	The End of the Games	23
9	And Today?	25

1 Death

Death stared him in the face.
He couldn't fight any more.
He lay on his back
on the sand.
His sword was broken.
He had lost his shield.

His enemy stood over him,
holding a sword to his throat.

These could be his last few seconds of life.
The sun beat down.
The crowd roared.

He had fought hard.
The sand was spotted with blood.
His own blood
and the blood of his enemy.

Some of the crowd roared for him to live.
Others roared for him to die.

His enemy turned
to look at the Emperor.
The Emperor slowly put out his hand.
His thumb pointed . . . down.

The crowd went quiet.
The man looked up at the sky –
the last thing he would ever see.
His enemy pushed the sword home.
The man's life-blood ran out on to the sand.

2   The Games

A few thousand years ago in ancient Rome,
scenes like this were common.
Crowds gathered to watch men
fight to the death.
These men were called gladiators.
The fights were called the 'Games'.

The Games were very popular
with the Romans.
In a way, they are still popular with us.
We enjoy films about them.
Films like *Ben Hur*
and *Gladiator*.

Gladiator stars Russell Crowe.
It is about a Roman general, Maximus,
who falls out with the new Emperor.
His family are killed
and he himself is made a slave.

Gladiator was an instant hit when it was released.

He joins a training school for gladiators.
He becomes a gladiator
and fights in the Games.

The film shows Maximus as a hero –
but it also shows how cruel and dangerous
the Games were.

In real life, the Games were even more
cruel and dangerous than in the film.
A gladiator's life was a short one.
Most people who fought in the Games
did not want to be gladiators.
They had no choice.

So how did it all begin?

3 How it all began

It all began about three thousand years ago
in ancient Rome.
The Games were first put on at funerals.
When a rich nobleman died,
his slaves had to fight to the death
at his funeral.
This was so he would have soldiers
to look after him in the next world.

People who went to the funerals enjoyed
watching the fights.
In fact, the fights became more important
than the funerals.

Soon, rich men began to put on Games
when they were still alive.
They made their slaves fight
and people came to watch.

It was a good way for rich men
to make themselves popular with the people.
Everyone loved the Games.
Except for those who had to fight in them.

Huge crowds came to watch the Games.
They had to build special stadiums for them.
The stadiums were called 'amphitheatres'.
The space in the middle
where the gladiators fought
was called the arena.

Soon, every Roman town
had its own amphitheatre.
Not just Rome itself,
but all over the Roman Empire.
In Italy, in France,
in Spain, in Greece,
in North Africa
and in Britain.

You can still see the remains
of Roman amphitheatres in Britain today.

4 Law and Order

It wasn't just slaves
who were made to fight in the Games.
As time went on,
the Games were used
more and more often
to punish criminals.
The Games were a way of keeping
law and order.
If you broke the law,
you would be sent to fight as a gladiator.
Women as well as men
were sent to fight as gladiators.

They had to fight to the death
against other gladiators.
Or they had to fight to the death
against wild animals.
Lions and tigers,
bears and crocodiles.

Sometimes, if a gladiator had fought very bravely,
the crowd would shout for them to be freed.
Then the giver of the Games –
the Emperor, or a wealthy noble –
might grant the gladiator their freedom.
But this didn't happen very often.
Most gladiators died.
They were killed by other gladiators
or torn apart by wild beasts.

The crowds enjoyed watching these scenes.
It was good to see criminals being punished.
No one felt sorry
for the men and women sent to die in this way.

Christians were sometimes sent to die
in the Games.
The Romans didn't trust Christians –
how could someone who is loyal to Jesus
also be loyal to the state of Rome?
So every now and again
the Romans turned on the Christians.
They threw them to the lions.

5 The Professionals

Not all gladiators
were slaves or criminals.
Some were free men.
Why would anyone choose
such a dangerous job?
It was probably mostly men
who had lost their money.
Fallen on hard times.
Such a man could choose
to become a professional gladiator.

To do this, he would have to join
a training school.
He would be trained to fight.
He would have to swear to obey his trainer.
After that, he was no longer free.
He had to fight in the Games
whenever he was told to.

There were different types of fighters.
Some had heavy armour and swords.
Others had little or no armour,
a spear and a net.
There were fights between
these different types of gladiators.
There were also chariot fights.

Every time a gladiator won a fight,
he was given a cash prize.
If a gladiator was brave and strong,
he could make a good living –
for a while.

Successful gladiators became public heroes.
They were given crowns for bravery.
They were worshipped by young girls –
just as pop stars are today.

Graffiti on the walls of ancient Roman towns
show the names of gladiators.
Some houses had pictures and mosaics
of gladiators –
just as we have posters of pop stars
or footballers today.

If a gladiator won lots of fights
and became popular,
he was given a wooden club.
This meant he was free.
He no longer had to fight in the Games.

But most gladiators came to the same end.
They died in the arena.
Their life-blood ran out on to the sand,
while the crowd roared.

6   Wild Animals

As well as people,
many animals died in the Games.
The Romans loved to see fights
between wild beasts,
and fights between beasts and people.

Animals were brought from
all over the Empire, especially from Africa.
Big animals like elephants,
rhinos and crocodiles were very popular.
So were fierce animals,
like lions, tigers and bears.

Harmless animals like ostriches
were used, too.
The Emperor Commodus
appeared in the arena
and killed ostriches in front of the crowd.
He shot them through the neck with arrows.

Most of all, the crowds loved
fights between fierce animals.
The poet Martial wrote of a fight
between a lion and a tiger.
'A tigress fiercely tore a wild lion apart.
She wouldn't have dared do this
when she lived in the forests.
Since she has lived among humans,
she has become fiercer.'

Very large numbers of animals were killed.
At Games given by Julius Caesar,
40 elephants and 400 lions were killed.

Today, we are shocked
to think of so many animals
being killed for sport.
In Roman times, it was different.
There were still lots of wild animals
in Europe, Asia and Africa.
Killing them made life safer.

Perhaps we wouldn't be so keen
to protect the tiger,
if we had tigers stalking around
outside our town!

7   The Colosseum

The biggest of all the Roman
amphitheatres was the Colosseum.
It was built in Rome
nearly two thousand years ago.

It could hold 50,000 spectators –
45,000 seated and 5000 standing.
It is 513 metres wide
and 287 metres long.
The walls are nearly 40 metres high.

It is a very grand building.
There are 76 arches on the ground floor
for spectators to enter through.
There are arches on every floor to let in light.
The outside is decorated with
columns and carvings.

The Colosseum in Rome today.

The Colosseum took nine years to build.
It was started by the Emperor Vespasian
in AD 71 as a gift for the people of Rome.
Building amphitheatres was a good way
for Emperors to make themselves popular.
However, Vespasian died before
it was finished.
It was finished in AD 80,
when Titus was Emperor.

To mark the opening of the Colosseum,
Titus held Games that lasted for 100 days.
There were massive fights
with hundreds of gladiators every day.
Thousands of gladiators died.
Nine thousand animals were killed
during the 100 days.
Every day, the Colosseum
was packed with spectators.

The seating was strictly ordered.
On the ground floor,
in the middle, sat the emperor.
This was the seat with the best view.

The emperor could see everything –
and everyone could see the emperor.
The richest and most important nobles
also sat on the ground floor.

The less important you were,
the further away you sat.
Women and slaves sat
right up on the top floor.

The Colosseum was built to last.
It is still standing –
you can see it in Rome today.

8   The End of the Games

It may seem strange to us
that the Romans loved the Games so much.
Why didn't they think it was cruel?
Why didn't anyone protest?

In fact, a few people did protest.
Some Roman writers complained
about the Games.
The writer Seneca didn't like them.
He said it was bad for people
to see so much killing and bloodshed.
He said it made people cruel.

The Christian writer, St Augustine
also disliked the Games.
He said they made the crowd mad,
drunk with bloodshed.

Both these writers thought the Games
were bad for the people watching.
No one had much pity
for the gladiators themselves.
If they were slaves,
people thought they didn't matter.
If they were criminals,
people thought they deserved it.
If they were professionals,
they had chosen it themselves.

As time went on, however,
more people objected to the Games.
When the Roman Empire became Christian,
the Games ended.
In the fourth century AD,
the first Christian Roman Emperor,
Constantine, banned fights to the death.

9 And Today?

Today, we find the Games shocking.
We find it hard to understand
how civilised people
could enjoy watching gladiators
hacking each other to pieces.

But are we so different?
Today, we enjoy horror films,
full of killing and bloodshed.
We watch boxing matches
where there is a risk of death.
In Spain, people watch bullfights.

Bullfights are still held in Spain today.

Only 150 years ago,
we had public executions in this country.
If we still had them today,
probably many people
would go along to watch.

What if we had gladiators today,
who fought to the death,
as in Rome?
Would people go along to watch?

Would you?